NEW YORK

THE TRAVEL GUIDE FOR CHRISTMAS

Richard L. Stanley

CONTENTS

INTRODUCTION

Once again, Christmas is approaching, and people everywhere are busy making preparations for their unique takes on Christmas supper.

Christmas is a time for

- family get-togethers,

- strengthening relationships within the family,

- rekindling old friendships,

- gift-giving, and

- vacations.

Christmas is celebrated in many ways by Christians across the globe, each of whom observes their customs and beliefs.

The celebration of Jesus' birth comes first.

Its intended message of hope and peace is now overwhelmed by the tension that many people experience as they get ready for Christmas.

Is Christmas a season of stress?

Could the commercialization of the otherwise sacred festival be held responsible for the stress?

The majority of people nowadays are preoccupied with their jobs, thus planning for the holidays is often postponed until the very last minute.

Due to last-minute customers,
retailers,
department stores,
malls,
grocery stores, and
supermarkets

are overflowing at the seams only a few days before Christmas.

Presents used to be more straightforward, but nowadays, especially among younger people, individuals are pickier about the gifts they give and receive.

Christmas festivities now include several parties. Parties are held by community organizations, friends, and coworkers, as well as at work.

Attending parties over the holidays has become socially required since it is almost difficult to decline an invitation.

Even while gatherings are fun, the true spirit of the Christmas holiday is somehow obscured by all the commotion.

When given money, chocolates, fruits, a new pair of shoes, or new clothing in the past, youngsters were happy.

The newest video gaming devices, mobile phones, and high-tech toys are now in great demand among kids.

WHAT DOES CHRISTMAS MEAN TO OTHERS?

There are still many individuals, both young and old, around the globe who have a different understanding of what the holiday season entails, even though many have all but forgotten what it entails.

Here are a few fundamental definitions:

- It is to honour the birth of the Creator, not to exchange gifts.

- to give to those without homes, to care for those who do, and to commemorate the birth of Jesus.

- It is a period of family time.

- to give God praise.

- The holiday is all about enjoying yourself, spending time with family, and not having to go to work or school.

- assisting those in need to enjoy Christmas

- It is a time for spending time with family and giving back to the neighbourhood.

Seeing the actual fervour and allure of the holiday season through the eyes of youngsters.

Now is the moment to consider what matters most in life.

To share love and aid other people.

It involves expressing appreciation and compassion.

it's time to make people smile.

The main point is obvious.

Christmas means spending extra time with family, being thankful and caring, giving and cheering others up, and remembering the Savior, Jesus Christ, who was born.

These are the common connotations of the holiday season for many people, but there is something more that makes it more exciting and loving: nothing else than taking a trip with one's family to a location where there are Christmas celebration vibes.

How about making things more different this time around by going for a special Family Vacation Rather Than Giving Gifts?

Here are some excellent reasons to go on a family vacation this year rather than exchanging presents, whether you want to lessen clutter or simply have fun!

-It's a significant choice to choose for a family vacation over providing presents, particularly if your family has never done it before.

There are methods to reach a compromise so that everyone in your family may still enjoy a holiday without gifts.

Downsizing your gift-giving along with a family vacation is an easy way to ease into the tradition, whether you choose to stick to a smaller budget for gift purchases, decide to only give handmade gifts to each other, or follow a simpler tradition this holiday season (one gift you need, one gift you wear, and one gift you read, for example).

Christmas travel benefits Less clutter in your home
You'll need to find a home for all the new items you buy for your kids once the presents have been opened and the tree has been stored.

After the holidays are gone, your house will likely be crowded with new clothing and toys. Why not buy a family-friendly event instead of blowing your Christmas cash on goods that will simply add to the clutter in your home? Your family room won't be crowded during a vacation, but it will be with a load of new toys.

-*Lower Waste*

Consider the trash generated by giving those new toys to your children in addition to the amount of room they will take up.

There is a lot of garbage produced throughout the Christmas season, including wrapping paper, ribbons, boxes, and gift bags.

Consider who will be responsible for cleaning up the mess of toy boxes and wrapping paper after the holidays, in addition to the additional trash.

Consider giving your family the gift of a vacation rather than purchasing brand-new items for your children and packaging them to place under the tree.

This Christmas, you won't need to use any unnecessary wrapping paper to present that gift.

-*Traveling is Educative*

Whatever location you choose for your vacation, there will undoubtedly be some educational features there.

Your children will have the opportunity to see nature and animals during a winter beach holiday.

Your kids will enjoy seeing the fascinating historical places of your chosen city.

Family vacation offers the opportunity to encounter different cultures, sample new cuisines, and discover new things about themselves and their family members in addition to the educational locations to view.

-More family time spent together

The focus of the Christmas season is family and love.

With a pleasant family excursion, make the most of the holiday mood.

A family vacation allows everyone to spend time together for an extended length of time without the usual distractions that often cause us to grow apart.

You can be sure that your family will spend a lot of quality time together on vacation no matter where you travel or what you do.

-Create Profound Family Memories

The interest your child has in toys and games is ephemeral. The gifts kids have requested for Christmas this year may be enough to keep them occupied until the next holiday.

However, a vacation is something they will always have. Family vacations can help your children establish enduring relationships with one another that they may carry into adulthood.

Your family will chat about those experiences at dinnertime for years to come.

-Removes the Emphasis on Material Things

Children may so easily get engrossed in the hedonistic parts of the Christmas season.

Your children are constantly reminded that they need material possessions throughout the holiday season thanks to ads for all the new Christmas toys and conversations among their pals about their wish lists.

However, taking a vacation rather than buying them unnecessary gifts this year can help them appreciate the significance of the occasion.

They may strengthen their relationships with their family members and make memories that will last a lifetime rather than obtaining material stuff.

CHRISTMAS IN NEW YORK: HOLIDAY ACTIVITIES IN NEW YORK

It seems like every memorable holiday film or experience we have involves New York City in some way.

Are you looking for activities in New York City?

We are all aware that arranging a vacation to New York City might be difficult.

There is just so much to see that choosing what to concentrate on might be a very difficult issue.

So we made this book to guide you in making sure booking your vacation to New York is as very simple and easy.

DECEMBER'S WEATHER IN NEW YORK CITY

The onset of winter brings cooler temperatures to New York.

Daytime highs are around 43F (6C), while overnight lows are typically 32F. (0C).

Even though it won't be as chilly as January and February, you should still bundle up! In December, the average number of days with below-freezing temperatures is three (-8 C).

Despite the cold, a snowy Christmas seems improbable, despite how cold it is.

The average low temperature of 32F (0C) means that it is often not cold enough for snow to form.

In New York, December barely sees two days of snow every month on average.

Still, December typically has eight days of rain every month.

HOW TO PREPARE FOR DECEMBER IN NEW YORK

You must have a warm winter coat! In the winter, the majority of New Yorkers dress in down-filled jackets.

Bring caps, gloves, and a scarf, too.

Put on layers! Bringing basic layers is worthwhile (thermal clothing).

The health thermals from Uniqlo are a nice, less expensive choice.

Preserve your feet dry and toasty!

Streets may become soaked, slippery, and snowy for days if it rains or snows.

Boots for winter are necessary. Likewise, excellent, toasty socks.

When selecting boots, keep in mind that the sidewalks have been salted to melt the ice.

Leather boots may get stained by salt!.

New York City is fantastic!

Whether you are visiting New York City for the first time or the fifth time, this list of the best things to do will make your vacation memorable.

Before making a reservation, be careful to inquire about the current policies and hours of operation for each attraction. These days, everything is always changing.

Although all five of the city's boroughs are worthwhile seeing, we will concentrate on Manhattan since it is where most visitors start.

The must-do activities are listed at the top (particularly if this is your first visit), and the activities we think you can leave for a second or third visit are listed at the bottom.

For your convenience, pricing and Google map locations for each attraction are listed just for you.

- *National Memorial and Museum*

A trip to Ground Zero at One World Trade Center and the National Memorial and Museum is essential to understand the courage and tenacity of the New Yorkers.

A powerful monument now stands where the Twin Towers once stood.
At the foot of the twin buildings, two memorial reflection pools with names engraved onto the brickwork are there.

Skyscrapers surround the pools, demonstrating how New York has recovered and is now standing with optimism rather than hatred.

Every person should visit the 911 Memorial Museum.
The 1993 World Trade Center bombs and the damage caused by the September 11 attacks on the United States are shown within.

Whether you are visiting New York for the first time or not, in our opinion, it is one of those essential things to accomplish.

The National Memorial and Museum serves as a constant reminder that tragedies bring out the best in people, while mindless acts of violence only harm the innocent.

Museum and Memorial Included with Your New York Pass, $20 for Admission, or $40 for Admission and a Tour at the on-site ticket booths
Maps on Google Greenwich Street: 180 City

- *Hall of the Empire*

The New york Skyline at night is unlike any other city in the world.
in particular from above. The Empire State Building's ascent becomes one of the greatest things to do in New York as a result.

It used to be the tallest skyscraper in New York, but the new structure at World Trade Center now has that distinction.

Even still, the views of the city are stunning from here.

The Empire State Building is best visited at night, in our opinion,Till 2 AM, the viewing deck is accessible.

Going after midnight means that there are no crowds for you to struggle with while soaking in the neon lights blazing the metropolitan skyline.

You are advised to arriving early to beat the queues if you do want to see the Empire State Building throughout the day.

City Hall of the Empire Cost: $42 at the entrance or free with a New York Pass.
Maps on Google: 20 West 34th Street

- *Ascend to the rock's summit.*

Without seeing the Rockefeller Center and the Top of the Rock, in my view, no journey to New York is complete.

One of New York's greatest vistas may be seen here. Although I believe that the view of the skyline from the Top of The Rock is superior to that from the Empire State Building, the view of the latter is spectacular.

The view of New York City as seen from the top of the cliff is one that we have all seen in movies.

In addition, it's wonderful to go here since NBC Studios are located here.
You can watch the Today program outdoors in the morning, and if you want to make an effort, you can attempt to catch a Jimmy Fallon recording.

Make sure you get your Top of the Rock tickets in advance. During the busiest times, it may become quite busy.

Cost: $38 at the venue or free with a New York Pass.

Also included in the New York Pass are complimentary tours of Rockefeller Center. If not, it costs $25, and both must be reserved in advance.
Maps on Google: 30 Rockefeller Plaza\s4.
The Metropolitan Museum of Art

One of the nicest things you can do in New York if you want to include some culture is to visit the museums.

The most preferred museum in New York City is the Metropolitan Museum of Art.
The Metropolitan Museum has a lot to offer.

Highlights include

Van Gough's self-portrait,

Dante's Inferno, ruins,

a replica of the Sistine Chapel, and

an amazing Egyptian Display replete with mummies and ancient tombs.

It takes days to appreciate it all. You don't have to stay here for days, however, You'll have a fair understanding of what it has to offer within an hour or two.

People mean it when they say you could spend days visiting the Met.
Price: Free with a New York Pass.
$25 at the website of the Metropolitan *Museum of Art Google Maps location: 1000 Fifth Avenue, New York*

- ## *Visit the Statue of Liberty in the Morning*

The Statue of Liberty is one of the best sights to visit in New York, according to everyone you ask. We concur, but you must be dedicated and have the time. It consumes a significant portion of your day.

You may have to wait in line for the boat for hours if you visit New York at the height of the tourist season.

After that, Liberty Island is reached after a 15-minute ride from Battery Park.

When you get to the Statue of Liberty, you may schedule a time to go to the statue's summit, after which you can tour Lady Liberty and take in the vistas of Manhattan.

Visit a fantastic museum where the actual flame is on display.
If this is your first visit to New York, you should schedule some time to see it since it is both spectacular and priceless.

Free with a New York Pass, but there are no VIP or skip-the-line options available.

To get a paper ticket for the queue, you must enter the castle.

Maps on Google In Lower Manhattan, there is a national monument called Castle Clinton.
Ellis Island 6.

The Statue of Liberty and Ellis Island tours are often combined.

To learn about the background of immigration to New York, Take the stairs to the second level where you will see a wonderful collection of images chronicling the history of Ellis Island.
Included in the Statue of Liberty Tour price

To do lists in liberty city for All budgets

- *The Oculus*

Your attention will be attracted to the spectacular building known as the Oculus when touring the monument.

Doves fluttering from a child's hands are shown in the design of the interlocking,

bright white steel ribs that are hundreds of feet above the earth.

At the scene of a catastrophe, it instils a feeling of hope.
Since it is a major transit centre, you will likely get here via subway. It is one of the top free activities in New York, in our view.
Price: Free
Church Street, New york, according to *Google Maps. Observe The Vessel in Awe*

The Vessel at Hudson Yards is a magnificent piece of art that offers aspiring photographers their ideal opportunity to capture a picture fit for Instagram.

Make sure to include this on your list of enjoyable things to do in New York City.

This artwork, which is surrounded by striking buildings, leads you up a spiral staircase that has 2500 steps for views of the Hudson River and midtown.

Given that it is so distinctive, this was undoubtedly among the finest things to shoot in New York.

Free admission is available, but you must reserve a timed period at the kiosks in advance.

To avoid having to wait around, you are advised to arriving early.
Cost: Free, or $10 to enter whenever you want, Tickets may be bought at the booths next to The Vessel.
On their website, you may make reservations as far in advance as two weeks.

You are entitled to Free Tours of the Hudson Yards and the vessel with your New York Pass.

- ***The Hudson Yards Shopping District***

This area in midtown Manhattan is a great spot to spend the morning.

Once inside, you can see the vessel in more interesting detail. We can only speculate as to who lives in an apartment in this area since it is home to incredibly costly condominiums.

MUST-SEE NEW YORK ATTRACTIONS

- ***Free Bicycle Rental in Central Park***

One of my favourite spots in Manhattan is Central Park, and no trip to the city is complete without at least seeing there.

The Mall is a pedestrian route lined with elm trees where you can see street performers, visit monuments of

Hans Christian Anderson and

Alice in Wonderland,

have coffee by the pond, and snap pictures of the Bethesda Fountain.

Consider renting a bicycle if you only have a limited amount of time since Central Park is enormous.

Wheels will help you view everything quickly since there are so many sights to take in.

If you have more time, we've found that getting lost and simply wandering about Central Park is one of the greatest ways to explore it.

It is a terrific way to spend a few hours away from the hustle and bustle of Manhattan's streets since you will always arrive at a major street.

Horse-drawn carriages, pedicabs, strolling, and Central Park tours are other ways to explore Central Park.

- ***Observe John Lennon's memory at Central Park***

John Lennon is remembered in Strawberry Fields, which is a monument on Central Park's West Side.

Lennon spent a lot of time in this area of Central Park since he resided just across the street at the Dakota (where he was also shot in the front).

In the middle of the route is a circular mosaic that resembles a record and has the word "imagine" inscribed into it.

Travellers in droves have gathered there to take pictures of the well-known monument, so go early in the morning.
use Google Maps To Strawberry Fields.

- ### *Go to Grand Central Terminal via subway*

The biggest railway station in the world, this is more than just your typical train station.

In addition to being a significant hub, it is one of New York City's most stunning structures.

- ***Consider a Boat Tour***

If you don't want to go to the Ellis or Liberty islands themselves, we advise going on a boat cruise to view New York from the ocean.

With boats to Governors Island, New York City Water Taxis across the channel, and Liberty Island Boat Tours (where you don't have to get off), there are many opportunities to go out on the Hudson River in New York.
Taking the Staten Island Ferry is the most cost-effective method to see the Statue of Liberty and Manhattan up close.

It travels through New York Harbor every day of the week. If you have some time, spend an hour or two exploring Staten Island, or just enjoy the sights.

- ***New York Public Library***

I hear you when you remark, "Who visits the library anymore?" But the Stephen A. Schwarzman Public Library in New York City is unique.

This edifice, which dates back to the 1800s, is quite stunning.

The beautifully refurbished Rose Reading Room alone makes the journey worthwhile and is free to see.

This is something you definitely won't want to miss if you like architecture.

The second-largest library in the world is the subject of free visits every day at 11 a.m.
5th Avenue at 476
St. Patrick's Cathedral, number thirty

They are filled with so much history. One of the most well-known and historic churches in the country is Saint Patrick's Cathedral in New York.

This is another to add to the list if, you only visit tourist attractions like the Vatican, Notre Dame, and the Koln Cathedral.

Getting there using Google Maps

- ***Eat Pasta in Little Italy 31.***

There isn't a cooler Italian neighbourhood anyplace in the globe, in my opinion (outside of Italy).

This area of the city has managed to preserve some of its historical features. Even the garland hanging over the streets is ornamented with white and green stripes, which are the national colours of Italy.

Some restaurants in Little Italy date back to the 1800s, and the neighbourhood has so far resisted gentrification (at least for now).

So stop in for a bite to eat and emulate New york's most well-known Italians.

Food is the greatest way to experience this region. To fully experience Little Italy's culture, enrol in a food tour.
A Good Start may be found on Mulberry Street and Canal Street.

- ### *View a Few Broadway Shows*
If you like live performances, you already know that seeing a Broadway musical is among the best things to do in New York City.
Times Plaza, which is located in the centre of Broadway, has marquee billboards advertising the newest Broadway musicals on streets that project out from the square.

There is no better way to watch your favourite actor than to go see them in a play on Broadway, where movie stars often demonstrate their acting prowess.

The New York Pass app informs you of the discounts available while you are in the city. Make sure to reserve your seats in advance, particularly if you want to see one of the more well-known performances.

- Check out The **Lincoln Center's cultural offerings**

The Metropolitan Opera House, David H. Koch Theatre, and David Geffin Hall are all located at the Lincoln Center.

The New York Philharmonic,

The Metropolitan Opera, and

The New York City Ballet

are all located there. So this is one of the greatest opportunities to spend an evening in high society.

The scene in the movie Moonstruck when Cher and Nicolas Cage visit the Met comes to mind whenever we think about opera.

It's a holiday tradition, so if you're in New York at this time of year, we recommend seeing The Nutcracker at the Lincoln Center! And this could be a good time to watch the ballet if you've always wanted to.

Lincoln Center Plaza, New York 34

THE BEST WAYS TO SAVE MONEY IN NEW YORK CITY

To see all the biggest New York City attractions, It cost $199 for a three-day ticket. Almost all of the best things to do in New York, including tours, are accessible via it.

If you want to get a feel for the city and take a tour, it also includes a hop-on, hop-off bus that you can use to get from one region to another for no additional cost. However, the subway is quicker.

The tourist bus, however, is the ideal choice if you are not used to utilizing metropolitan metros.

ACCOMMODATIONS IN NEW YORK

There are several fantastic hotels in New York.

from the upscale lodgings close to Central Park to the more budget-friendly lodgings on the upper east side.

Everyone can find something. It's best to pick your lodging after deciding where you want to go exploring first, then basing your hotel choice on that.

Midtown is one of the greatest spots to stay if you're a first-time visitor since you'll be right in the middle of everything.

The only downside is that it may grow quite pricey.

Consider the Lower East Side or Upper Westside if you're on a tight budget and make use of one of the greatest metro systems in the world.

Although it can take a bit longer to move about the city, it will save you a ton of money.

HOTELS NEAR TIMES SQUARE THAT ARE PERFECT FOR ALL BUDGETS

Many individuals believe that to live in New York on an affordable budget or to find peace, they must be far from the city's bustle.

- ## *Best Accommodations Near Times Square*

To assist you in making travel arrangements, we offer a detailed overview of Where to Stay in New York City - Top Places and Hotels For All Budgets.

- ## *Times square*

The enormous metropolis of New York has several boroughs and neighbourhoods.

Queens, and Brooklyn are great hotels, but Times Square is still the best. When staying at a hotel near Times Square, you may easily navigate the streets of New York since it is a walking city.

Favourite top ten sights in Times Square:

- Times Square, which is a sight in and of itself

- Rockefeller Center;

- Radio City Music Hall

- Bryant Park

- Broadway

- Hell's Kitchen

- Fifth Avenue shopping

- Bloomingdales

- MoMA

- *InterContinental Times Square*

A luxurious hotel, which is located at *300 West 44th Street in New York*.

InterContinental Hotels are the top of the line in the IHG family.
The InterContinental Hotel Times Square, which sits between the Times Square District and Hell's Kitchen, is absurdly close to Times Square

Directly across the street is Birdland, a well-known pub where Broadway performers congregate after performances.

The Intercontinental is elegant and stylish as well as serene and calm.

With turndown service, doormen who can call taxis for you, and valet parking for your car, it offers all the conveniences of a high-end hotel.

THANKSGIVING DINNER OPTIONS IN NEW YORK

- ## *Kimika*

The Feast of the Seven Fishes may not be served traditionally at this innovative Japanese-Italian fusion restaurant, but it's sure to be a tremendous delight.

Shareable, pescatarian delicacies like the Japanese-inspired

fritto misto,

grilled hamachi collar with salsa verde, and

saffron pasta with shellfish, nduja, and shiso

will be included in this family-style feast, which costs $120 per person.

The intriguing cocktail menu is worth paying special attention to (chamomile negroni).

Resy lets you make reservations.

New York, NY 10012, 40 Kenmare St.

- **Jungsik**

This Christmas season, if you're truly seeking to treat yourself, this one is a special recommendation,

a contemporary Korean restaurant with two Michelin stars.

On December 24 and 25, this upscale restaurant is offering a decadent 11-course tasting menu for $395 per person.

Expect opulent dishes like

Alaskan black cod,

grilled Iberico de Bellota, and

Spanish Carabinero prawns with caviar.

There are also optional wine and Champagne pairings, depending on how fancy you want to go.

New York, NY 10013, **2 Harrison St.**

- ***Littlemad***

LittleMad, a newcomer to the NoMad restaurant scene, is presenting a special four-course dinner for $155 per person on Christmas Eve and Christmas Day, filled with caviar, truffles, and all of life's finest indulgences.

The menu offers dishes including crispy duck skin noodles, wagyu tartare, tiger prawns, and yellowtail with Asian pear and sesame sauce. For an extra $95 there is also an optional wine pairing.

New York, NY 10016; 110 Madison Avenue

- ### *Tiny's*

On Christmas Eve, a special holiday meal will be served at this very intimate Tribeca establishment nestled in a charming townhouse.

The three-course menu costs $85 per person and includes some delectable choices including

lobster tortellini,

pan-roasted halibut with Romanesco, and

filet mignon with potato gratin.

Even the young ones may partake in the celebrations thanks to a $25 kids' meal and an optional wine pairing.

New York, New York 10013, 135 W Broadway

- ***Rolo's***

Four former employees of Gramercy Tavern are behind this local eatery in Ridgewood, Queens, so you can be sure it will be excellent.

Rolo's is providing a special à with la carte menu for pick-up on December 23, ideal for your Christmas Eve party.

This is a terrific choice for those who aren't quite ready to eat inside but don't feel like cooking.
A full maple glazed ham,

brown butter pretzel parker house buns,

tomato garlic focaccia, and

cherry mascarpone chocolate almond cake

are just a few of the options available.

Address: *853 Onderdonk Avenue, Queens, NY 11385;*

- **Soogil**

On December 24 and 25, this East Village Korean restaurant will be open with a special Christmas menu that includes six courses for $158 per person including delicacies like

tuna tartare with Kaluga caviar,

gougères with foie gras mousse,

scallops with gochujang crust, and

beef Wellington with mushrooms.

A wine pairing and a uni and caviar dish are two more add-ons that are available.

On Resy, you may make reservations for heated indoor and outdoor meals.

New York, NY 10003; 108 E 4th St

- ***Jack & Charlie's***

On Christmas Eve, this brand-new restaurant by Chef Ed Cotton in the West Village will be open and offering its usual à la carte menu in addition to a few seasonal specialities, such as Dover sole meunière and red wine-braised goose with chestnuts.

The usual New American fare from this well-known restaurant, such as

oysters,

house-made pasta,

herb-roasted chicken, and

Tomahawk steak,

is of course available.

Location: *118 Greenwich Avenue, New York, NY 10011*;

Even though Saint Theo's in the West Village has only been operating for a few months, it already boasts some of the most sought-after tables in the city.

On Christmas Eve, Chef Ashley Rath (formerly of The Grill, Santina, and Dirty French) will serve diners a twist on the Feast of the Seven Fishes with a $205 tasting menu that includes specialities with a coastal Italian influence like

branzino,

caviar soup, and

grilled panettone with mascarpone for dessert.

New York, NY 10014; 340 Bleecker St.

- **Cote**

A spectacular Christmas Eve buffet is being prepared at an upmarket Korean steakhouse in Flatiron.

The "feast of the seven lumps of meat,"

a family-style buffet that costs $145 per person and includes

steak,

wagyu beef, and

lamb

along with a variety of sides like ban chan and savoury egg soufflé, is the highlight.

Of course, you could still choose from Cote's extensive à la carte menu, which includes all of the meats as well as shared appetizers such as Korean Bacon and Steak Tartare and Kimchi Wagyu Paella.

It also has a raw bar and caviar service.

New York 10010, 16 W 22nd St.

- ***a grill***

Christmas is the perfect occasion to treat yourself to a lavish supper, which leads us to The Grill, a popular eatery operated by Major Food Group that is located in the Seagram Building.

On Christmas Day, they're open and offering a special set dinner for $195 per person.

A family-style buffet of holiday appetizers, including

American ham and chestnut soup,

black truffle ravioli,

spit-roasted prime rib and sides, and

grasshopper bouche de noel, is served.

It will undoubtedly be a glamorous event worth dressing up for.

New York 10022, 99 E 52nd St;

- ***Carbone***

This iconic restaurant, which is a part of the Major Food Group, needs no introduction.

Christmas Day festivities at the popular Soho restaurant cost $195 a person and include some of your favourite Carbone classics in addition to holiday specials.

Consider roasted veal rack, burrata and caviar, and the renowned spicy rigatoni vodka.

Because these tables are sure to fill up quickly, make a reservation on Resy or sign up for the waitlist.

New York, NY 10012, 181 Thompson St.

- ### *Galbi Yoon Haeundae*

This Midtown restaurant serves a modern interpretation of classic Korean BBQ dishes and will be operating on Christmas Eve with its regular menu in addition to providing hefty meal packages for pickup or delivery.

For three to four people, each package costs $160 and comes with

three pieces of *meat (Signature Marinated Short Rib, Prime Strip Loin, and Dry-Aged Prime Ribeye),*

soybean stew,

potato noodles,

lettuce Ssam wraps,

three orders of Ssamjang,

four Banchan sides, and

rice.
Send an email to *info@hudhospitality.com* to place a pre-order for delivery or pick-up between December 21 and December 24, starting now through December 19.

New York 10018, 8 W 36th St;

- **Oxalis**

A favourite spot for a special occasion is this local cafe in Crown Heights, which is close to Prospect Park.

This is because of the fairly priced, often changing, and creative tasting menu.

On Christmas Eve, they'll be presenting an eight-course, $160 feast that includes local duck and offers a beverage pairing as an option.

Brooklyn, New York 11238; 791 Washington Avenue

- **Barbuto**

On Christmas Eve, the renowned and recently renovated West Village Barbuto by Chef Jonathan Waxman will be open and offering a $125 menu of both Barbuto classics and festive seasonal embellishments.

The menu is yet to be determined, but we can only expect to see the legendary kale salad with Pecorino and breadcrumbs, the classic roast chicken with salsa verde, and some delectable seasonal plates of pasta.

New York, NY 10014; 113 Horatio St.

- ### *Kitchen ABC*

The long-time flatiron favourite ABC Kitchen by Jean-Georges Vongerichten will be offering a three-course prix fixe menu for $168 per person.

The menu will feature some of ABC's most cherished farm-to-table, seasonally-inspired dishes in addition to a few holiday specials.

Choose from dishes like

peekytoe crab toast,

poppy seed-crusted fish from the Faroe Islands,

stracciatella with black truffle and pizza Bianca, and

wagyu beef tenderloin with potato gnocchi and gingerbread cake.

New York 10003 35 E 18th St

- ***Faun***

This Italian-themed restaurant in Prospect Heights is open on Christmas Eve and offers a special Christmas four-course prix-fixe menu for $125 per person with an extra $45 for a wine pairing.

There are many choices to please any kind of palette,

but some standouts include duck breast in mole Amarillo and pasta with lobster, fennel, and house-made focaccia bread.

Brooklyn, New York 11238 606 Vanderbilt Avenue

The Feast of the Seven Fishes is being reimagined for Christmas Eve at Scampi, a seaside Italian restaurant in Flatiron.

The supper is served family style and costs $95 per person. Some of the highlights are

octopus "fried rice" with farro,

bomba, and pancetta,

mafaldini scampi with shrimp,

garlic butter, and breadcrumbs, and

tuna acqua pazza with tomato and Calabrian chillies.

New York, New York 10011, 30 W 18th St

- ### *Meadowsweet*

On Christmas Eve, this Williamsburg restaurant with a Michelin star will serve a three-course meal for $85.

The Christmas menu at Meadowsweet has a wide variety of dishes to suit every taste, but some standouts include roasted heritage pig, duck breast with mole poblano, and seared bay scallops with savoy cabbage and black trumpet mushrooms.

On request, a vegan or vegetarian meal may be created for anyone with dietary requirements.

Brooklyn, New York 11211, 149 Broadway

- ***Limone House***

Eating a dish of fresh pasta at the southern Italian restaurant Casa Limone could well be a close second.

This beautiful restaurant is a perfect place to end your holiday outings since it is close to the Rockefeller Center Christmas Tree and Saks Fifth Avenue's colourful window displays.

On Christmas Eve, the restaurant will be open, and in addition to its normal menu, patrons may savour a cup of Italian hot chocolate and a piece of Panettone, the country's iconic holiday sweet bread.

New York 10017, 20 E 49th St

- *Olmstead*

For those who prefer the luxuries of a restaurant dinner in the comfort of their own home, this Park Slope institution is collaborating with sister restaurant Maison Yak to provide a take-out Christmas feast all weekend.

The $500 family-style bundle, which serves four people, is really powerful.

The Asian-inspired menu will include

black truffle short rib pot pie,

Christmas papaya salad with freshly baked bread, and

honey mustard glazed duck terrine.

And that's just the beginning. To have your order ready for Christmas Eve or Christmas Day pickup, place it before December 21.

Brooklyn, New York 11238; 659 Vanderbilt Avenue

- ***South Hotel***

With its seasonal, New American cuisine and "live fire" cooking, which uses charcoal, wood, and smoke, Sweetbriar Chef Bryce Shuman's newest establishment in the Park South Hotel is quickly establishing quite a name.

For a three-course prix-fixe menu with sharing sides that includes

butternut soup,

applewood smoked ham,

salmon mi cuit with horseradish cream,

rosemary roasted potatoes, and more,

make reservations at Sweetbriar for both Christmas Eve and Christmas Day.

New York, NY 10016, 127 E 27th St

HOLIDAY DRIVE-THRU LIGHT DISPLAYS IN NY AND NJ (PLUS, A FEW YOU CAN SEE ON FOOT)

Spending time with family and friends over the holidays is one of the nicest aspects of the season (after all the delicious food, of course).

And although we're huge fans of time-honoured customs like gift exchanging and watching Christmas movies, we advise beginning a brand-new holiday tradition this year by visiting one of these joyous drive-through Christmas light displays in the New York and New Jersey region.

No car? No issue. We have included a few no-wheels-needed Christmas light experiences around New York City.

So go ahead and gather your loved ones, a tin of seasonal cookies, and get ready to see an incredible show of Christmas happiness. This time of year!

- ***Festival of the Winter Lanterns in Roslyn, New York***

This 20-acre drive-through Christmas lights extravaganza is at the Nassau County Museum of Art in Roslyn, New York,

and it will undoubtedly get you in the holiday mood.

Don't be misled by the festival's name, A Bug's Night, since the exhibit is made up of colourful handcrafted lanterns, holiday lights, and projection mapping rather than real animals.

There are also two non-holiday lantern experiences on Staten Island and Queens, both of which remain open until January.

- *In Hammonton, New Jersey, Didonato's Magical Holiday Express*

Look no further than DiDonato's Magical Holiday Express if the Polar Express is one of your favourite holiday movies.

Get on a train, travel through countless Christmas lights, and meet the real Saint Nick.

The price of admission also includes a gift from Santa, story time and photos with Mrs Claus, a holiday movie tent, and much more.

Tickets may be bought online or at the door, although they tend to sell out fast.

open through December 30th.

- ***Magic Of Lights In Wantagh, New York***

With two miles of cheery and sparkly Christmas sceneries, Jones Beach State Park is once again home to one of Long Island's most well-liked light displays.

You'll pass a 200-foot light tunnel, moving snowmen, a Victorian hamlet, and an enchanting forest as you travel through Magic of Lights.

Visit the North Pole so that children (and adults!) may leave letters for Santa Claus using a preset template.

From November 19 until January 2, it will be accessible.

- ***The Winter Wonderland in Westchester New York's Valhalla***

Visit Westchester's Winter Wonderland to see well-known Christmas characters, a spinning tunnel, soaring candy canes, sparkling snowballs, and an elf playground.

What's best? A live Santa will be available for you to wave to while driving around in the privacy of your car and listening to a customized holiday playlist.

The event has a pre-sale ticket requirement and runs until January 2nd.

- ***Lights, Love, and Peace New York's Bethel***

Peace, Love & Lights, an annual Christmas event presented at the Bethel Woods Center for the Arts, is back and better than ever.

The 1.7-mile-long show includes new themed zones like New York and Holidays Around the World, as well as cheery attractions like a 120-foot twinkling tunnel, snowflake alley, and candy cane lane.

The drive-thru is available until January 2nd, and it takes roughly 30 minutes.

- ***Sesame Place's A Very Furry Christmas in Langhorne, Pennsylvania***

Although officially outside of New York or New Jersey, this location is nonetheless well worth the trek.

It takes 90 minutes to go to A Very Furry Christmas at Sesame Place from New York City, where you can spend the holidays with your favourite characters.

A 30-foot lit tree, a new Christmas Family Fun Zone, and a meet & greet with Santa turn the park into a winter paradise for the holidays.

From November 20 until January 2nd, the event is open.

- **_Christmas lights in Dyker Heights_**

Nobody does Christmas like Dyker Heights when it comes to the holiday spirit.

One of the greatest Christmas light displays in the nation can be seen in Brooklyn if you have access to a vehicle.

Homes go all out, decking their lawns with tens of thousands of sparkling lights, life-size snowmen, reindeer, and Santas everywhere.

The ideal field trip for keeping youngsters entertained or simply getting in the Christmas mood.

- ***Glow Nyberg in New York's Bronx***

The New York Botanical Garden's NYBG GLOW, now in its second year, will include more light shows than ever before.

The 1.5-mile, vibrant experience includes quirky installations, brilliant LED lights, and illuminated plant tales.

Additionally, guests may add on an evening visit to the Holiday Train Show, where miniature trains zoom past famous New York sites, or they can stop by the Bronx Night Market Holiday Pop-Up.

The event takes place on a few specific days between November 24 and January 22nd.

- **_Winter Wonderlights In East Brunswick, New Jersey_**

WinterWonder Lights puts a local family-owned company up and centre with enormous holiday-themed displays and over a million lights can be seen.

Get in your automobile and travel through a half-mile-long display of joyful animated lights honouring Kwanzaa, Hanukkah, Diwali, and Christmas.

The event is available for online ticket purchases and runs from November 25 through January 2nd.

- ***Demarest Farms' Orchard of Lights in Hillsdale, New Jersey***

Demarest Farms, an autumn favourite, changes into a joyful and stunning display of lights and seasonal activities over the holiday season.

You may take a guided drive-thru tour of the 32 acres of light displays at The Orchard of Lights while listening to your favourite Christmas music on a nearby radio station.

After the tour, take photographs with Santa and enjoy some hot chocolate and s'mores while listening to his singing reindeer.

Open from November 23 to January 9th, reservations are required online.

- ***Holiday   Light   Show   in Riverhead New York's Calverton***

For a can't-miss drive-thru experience, pack a bag with your favourite holiday sweets and travel to the Riverhead Holiday Light Show.

Tune your radio to a synchronized playlist and sing along as you travel the mile-long path.

The performance is available from November 19 through December 31 and begins at 5 p.m. every night. For other sites in New York and New Jersey, see their website.

- ***Light Show for Christmas at Skylands Stadium New Jersey's Augusta***

The Skylands Stadium Christmas Light Show is the best venue to join in on the holiday excitement.

You may stop at the outdoor Christmas village and enjoy

ice skating,

pictures with Santa,

carnival rides,

a s'mores station, and much more

after driving past more than 2 million lights. For those in need of "adult drinks," there is even a winter beer garden.

From November 24 through January 9th, it is open.

- ***Bronx Zoo Holiday Lights In Bronx, New York***

Bring your hot chocolate and winter jackets and visit the Bronx Zoo for a joyous light display with an animal theme.

Holiday decorations, colourful tunnels, immersive light shows, and more than 260 lanterns depicting various animal and plant species are all included in this walk-through experience.

Additional events include seasonal trains, stilt walkers, costumed characters, and ice carving demonstrations. From November 19 to January 9th, open on certain days

wishing you all a wonderful Merry Christmas and a prosperous New Year.

Made in the USA
Monee, IL
10 October 2022

15609503R00046